15 WAYS TO
Live Longer
AND Healthier

STUDY GUIDE

Also by Joel Osteen

JOEL OSTEEN

#1 *New York Times* Bestselling Author

15 WAYS TO
Live Longer
AND Healthier

LIFE-CHANGING STRATEGIES
for Greater Energy, a More Focused Mind, and a Calmer Soul

STUDY GUIDE

Faith Words

New York • Nashville

FaithWords
Hachette Book Group
1290 Avenue of the Americas, New York, NY 10104
faithwords.com
twitter.com/faithwords

First Edition: October 2023

FaithWords is a division of Hachette Book Group, Inc. The FaithWords name and logo are trademarks of Hachette Book Group, Inc.

The publisher is not responsible for websites (or their content) that are not owned by the publisher.

The Hachette Speakers Bureau provides a wide range of authors for speaking events. To find out more, go to hachettespeakersbureau.com or email HachetteSpeakers@hbgusa.com.

Literary development: Lance Wubbels Literary Services, Bloomington, Minnesota.

ISBN: 9781546005070 (trade pbk.)

Printed in the United States of America

LSC-C

Printing 2, 2023

Contents

Introduction

We are delighted that you have chosen to use this study guide that was written as a companion to *15 Ways to Live Longer and Healthier*. God created us to live a healthy, abundant, joyful, faith-filled life. He destined us to be confident, to be free, to be positive, and to be happy. He promises to give us strength for every day. He didn't create us to drag through the day, to be worn out by problems, discouraged and depressed by disappointments, even sick physically because we're living so stressed out, uptight, and worried. But it's easy to get so focused on what's wrong in our life, what we don't have, and how big our obstacles are that we leak out our joy and passion for living.

Research has shown that if you go through life in a negative frame of mind, always worried, full of fear, carrying emotional wounds and past guilt, it will weaken the production of the natural killer cells that your immune system creates to attack and destroy abnormal cells that cause disease, making you more susceptible to sickness. On the other hand, people who are happy and have a positive outlook develop more of those natural killer cells than the average person. When you stay full of joy, when your soul is healthy, your immune system functions at its peak performance level, just as God intended. You'll increase your brain activity and creativity, which can help you overcome challenges in difficult times. You'll reduce the stress hormone and increase production of the human growth hormone, also known as the "youth hormone," which slows down the aging process and keeps you looking younger and fresher.

The thoughts and questions addressed in this study guide will provide you with life-changing strategies to live with more energy, vitality, and happiness than you've ever imagined—not just for a week, or a month, but for the rest of your life. You'll discover that "a cheerful mind works healing," and that God has given you everything you need to live healthy and whole. You just have to do your part and tap into the promises of God and those things that breathe new hope into your heart and new vision into your spirit.

This study has been created so that it lends itself to self-study or personal development as well as small-group study or discussion, say in a care group or book club setting. Whichever the purpose you have in mind, you'll find great opportunity to personally be blessed as you take time to study and meditate on God's Word.

The format of each chapter is simple and user-friendly. For maximum benefit, it is best to first read the corresponding chapter from *15 Ways to Live Longer and Healthier*, and then work your way through the chapter in this study guide. The majority of the questions are personal, and taking the time to read through the chapters in the book and think through how each question can affect your life will give the study immediate personal application.

If you decide to use this study guide in a small group study, the most effective way is to go through each chapter on your own as preparation before each meeting. Take some time to read the relevant portions of text and to reflect on the questions and how they apply to you. This will give your group study depth and make the sessions more productive for all.

Because of the personal nature of this study, if you use it in a group setting or on a retreat, remember that confidentiality, courtesy, and mutual respect lay the foundation for a healthy group. A small group should be a safe place for all who participate. Don't let your conversations leave the small group. A small group is not a place to tell others what they should have done or said or think, and it's not a place to force opinions on others. Commit yourselves to listening in love to one another, to praying for and supporting one another, to being sensitive to their perspectives, and to showing each participant the grace you would like to receive from others.

CHAPTER ONE

A Healthy Soul

We spend a lot of time and energy taking care of our physical body. We try to eat right, exercise, get enough sleep, and take vitamins. That's all important. But we don't spend enough time taking care of our soul. We don't realize how much our emotions, our attitudes, and our thoughts are affecting us physically. If our soul is unhealthy, it's going to spill over to the physical.

1. The Scripture says, "Beloved, I pray that in every way you may succeed and prosper and be in good health, just as your soul prospers" (3 John 2 AMP). Describe the link between the health of our soul and our physical health. How does that show out in our day-to-day experience?

....

....

....

....

....

....

2. Write a list of some of the negative emotions and things we hang on to that often dominate our lives and make us sick. Which ones cause you the most trouble?

....

....

....

....

> *You can't take in all those toxins and not be poisoned.*

3. Describe at least one physical ailment you have had that you know was caused by stress or some other negative emotion. What was going on in your emotions, and what were you allowing to play in your mind? What was the outcome?

....

....

....

....

....

4. Do you look to others to keep your soul healthy, to fix you when you're down or stressed out or upset? Have you recognized that you are responsible for your own emotional well-being? In what ways do you, and in what ways have you not?

....

....

....

....

....

5. Is your soul healthy? Take some time to consider what is going on inside and write an honest review of what you find.

....

....

....

....

....

....

6. What valuable lesson can you take from the lady who was so easily angered by small disagreements with her husband? What destructive cycle was playing out in her thoughts and emotions over and over again?

....

....

....

....

....

7. Have you had an issue in your life where you found yourself asking, "Why am I like this? What's wrong with me?" Were you able to answer it, and was it resolved?

....

....

....

....

....

When you don't let go of hurts and emotional wounds, they never heal.

8. Pay attention to your inner life. Is there something that you've adapted to that is actually poisoning your soul and you're not recognizing it?

....

....

....

....

....

....

....

9. Why is it so important to heed the warning given in Hebrews 12:15? Have you experienced the harm that comes from a root of bitterness? Explain your answer.

....

....

....

....

....

....

10. Write out Proverbs 4:23 and begin to commit it to memory. Living in a world that brings so much against you, what practical steps can you take to do this?

....

....

....

....

....

....

11. Think for a moment about an issue that you've let take root and cause problems. How can you pull it up and get rid of it? How can you keep this from getting back in?

....

....

....

....

....

....

12. We tend to deal with the symptoms of problems, which never solve the problems. How does living from a place of faith get to the root of problems? Name some of the promises of God that will keep your faith strong to deal with the problems that impact you the most.

....

....

....

....

....

....

13. How does the story of the injured horse reflect what we often do with symptoms of an infection in our soul? Give an example of a time when you've tried to treat the symptom, but it just keeps recurring. What was the outcome?

Is there an infection in your soul that is keeping you from getting well?

....

....

....

....

....

....

14. At this point in the chapter, are you realizing that although you've tried to bury an issue and tell yourself it's not a problem, it really is a problem? If so, what is it?

....

....

....

....

....

....

....

15. The psalmist says, "Keep me from lying to myself" (Ps. 119:29 NLT). What makes that such a powerful prayer? Write a bold prayer that addresses the issues that you have been dealing with in this chapter.

....

....

....

....

....

....

16. Write down some of the favorite excuses you routinely use for why you get angry, bitter, or jealous. List any circumstances you use to excuse living worried and on edge. Make a declaration that you are pulling them up by the roots and not using them again.

....

....

....

....

....

....

17. What sin did David commit and then try to cover over and pretend everything was okay? What happened when he buried those negative toxins? Write down some of the thoughts that must have tormented his mind and heart with guilt and condemnation.

....

....

....

....

....

....

....

18. Read the entirety of Psalm 51. Write down the expressions of David's heart that stand out as the most important to you. Meditate on them and write them on your own heart for when you need them as David did.

....

....

....

....

....

....

....

19. The beauty of our God is that He is merciful to forgive our sins, to restore our soul and health, and to give us back the joy of our salvation. If your soul is broken and wounded from something you've done, or from something you've had done to you, you can be healed. Be honest with yourself, confess whatever you need to confess, and release whatever you need to release. Write it out as a prayer and ask God to bring the healing that you need, then receive it into your heart and give Him thanks and praise.

> *Don't believe the lies that it's too late, that you've made too many mistakes. Healing will come. Joy will come. Peace will come. Even now God is working to restore your soul.*

....

....

....

....

....

....

....

20. What lesson can you learn from the man whose rheumatoid arthritis had taken away his ability to play the piano?

....

....

....

....

....

21. Why must you forgive others in order to keep your own soul healthy? Is there someone you need to forgive and free yourself from the hurt? Do it now. Don't let them continue to hurt you by holding on to it.

....

....

....

....

....

22. "A merry heart does good, like medicine, but a broken spirit dries up the bones" (Prov. 17:22 NKJV). What can you start to do that will improve the health of your soul and keep you on the path to good success and good health?

....

....

....

....

....

CHAPTER TWO

Stay Positive Toward Yourself

The most important relationship you have is the relationship you have with yourself. Too many people don't like who they are. Instead of accepting themselves as made in the image of God, they focus on their faults, weaknesses, and failures, and wish they were different. They're not happy and don't have good relationships because they don't like themselves. If you don't get along with you, you're not going to get along with others.

1. What powerful life principle is found in Jesus' statement, "Love your neighbor as yourself" (Matt. 19:19)? What was your immediate response to the thought of loving yourself?

....

....

....

....

2. Would you say that "I discovered the enemy is me" is true for you? To what degree? Describe your thoughts.

....

....

....

....

3. What does "you can't give away what you don't have" mean? Why is that so important?

....

....

....

....

....

4. In what ways would you say you are waiting until you perform better to feel good about who you are? Do you beat yourself up about your weaknesses? Why is that detrimental?

....

....

....

....

....

5. God is changing us "from glory to glory" (2 Cor. 3:18 NKJV). What does that tell you about your weaknesses as well as where you are today?

> *Is your focus always upon how far you have to go?*

....

....

....

....

6. On a scale of 1 to 10, with 1 being "I don't like much about myself," and 10 being "I truly like myself," how would you grade yourself? What change in your thinking will help you improve in this area?

....

....

....

....

....

....

....

7. Take some time and reflect on whether your victories and accomplishments or your losses, mistakes, and flaws tend to be at the front of your mind. Describe some examples of the negative and positive images that are playing in your mind.

....

....

....

....

....

8. In what ways can you start to train your mind to focus on your positives? Name some of your victories and the ways you've succeeded in the past.

....

....

....

....

You can't become who you were created to be if you're negative toward yourself.

....

....

9. Write a description of your personality, temperament, and gifts. In what ways has God made you His unique creation?

....

....

....

....

....

....

....

10. "God has given you what you need to fulfill your destiny." Do you believe that statement is true, or do you compare yourself with others and feel inferior, not good enough or strong enough? In what ways do you think you have to be different or like someone else?

....

....

....

....

....

11. How can you start to feel comfortable in your own skin, comfortable in who God made you to be? What understanding will help you keep from going through life trying to be an imitation, copying someone else who you think is better?

....

....

....

....

....

....

12. How might what you've considered a weakness in your personality actually be a strength? Rather than fighting it or being unhappy about it, how can you start using it in a positive way?

....

....

....

....

....

13. When you criticize yourself, what are you actually criticizing? What different approach do you need to take?

....

....

....

....

....

14. How can saying "I did well" break strongholds in your thinking? Name some areas of your life where you need to say "I did well" and stop feeling badly about yourself.

....

....

....

....

....

15. The Scripture says, "Your faith may become effective by the acknowledgment of every good thing which is in you in Christ Jesus" (Philem. 6 NKJV). What can you start acknowledging about yourself, the good things God has put in you and is doing through you, that will make your faith effective and cause you to rise higher?

....

....

....

....

....

....

> *You should be your biggest fan. Nobody should think better of you than you.*

16. Do you tend to believe that if you think something good about yourself that it's not being humble? What is so wrong about that mind-set? How will that hold you back?

....

....

....

....

....

17. Many people have something negative from their past that they haven't forgiven themselves for, something the enemy holds over them with condemnation and guilt. Do you have a past failure or mistake that keeps you down on yourself? Describe it.

....

....

....

....

....

....

18. God says that "he has brought you into his own presence, and you are holy and blameless as you stand before him without a single fault" (Col. 1:22 NLT). What does that say about your past? Describe whether you see yourself without fault.

....

....

....

....

....

....

19. Read John 18:15–27. Peter's failure here was monumental. Why did Jesus choose him as a disciple in the first place, and how did this not disqualify him? What did Peter have to do, and what did it lead to?

....

....

....

....

....

....

20. Who were some other people in Scripture who made mistakes and failed and yet God used them in great ways? What did they do? What is God saying to you that He said to them?

....

....

....

....

....

....

21. Read Exodus 32. Based upon all that Aaron had seen God do, what made his failure and compromising so devastating? How was it possible that incident was not the end of service for Aaron? What is its message of hope for you today and for the future?

....

....

....

....

....

....

22. In a past question you were asked to describe a past failure or a season where you gave in to temptation and compromised. Are you allowing guilt and condemnation to hold you back? Write a prayer to the Lord, telling Him how you feel and thanking Him for His forgiveness and for making you holy, blameless, and without fault.

> *God has forgiven you, but you have to forgive yourself.*

....
....
....
....
....
....
....

23. Based on what you have learned in this chapter, take a moment and reflect on how you can start living every day loving yourself, being kind and merciful to yourself.

....
....
....
....
....
....
....
....
....
....
....
....

CHAPTER THREE

Choose to Be Happy

When we wake up in the morning, we get to choose how we're going to live that day. We can choose to live in faith, to be happy and expecting favor, or we can choose to live discouraged, defeated, and focused on our problems. Happiness doesn't happen automatically. It's a choice we have to make. You can't wait to see what kind of day it's going to be; you have to decide what kind of day it's going to be.

1. On a scale of 1 to 10, with 1 being that you live allowing circumstances to determine what kind of day you have, and 10 being that you choose to live happy no matter the circumstances, how would you grade yourself? Write an honest review.

....

....

....

....

....

....

2. The psalmist says, "Joy comes in the morning" (Ps. 30:5 NKJV). How might your life improve if you start out every morning believing and declaring that God is sending you a fresh supply of joy?

....

....

....

....

....

....

3. Write out Psalm 118:24 and commit this verse to memory. What is the difference between reporting on your life situation and making a declaration of faith about the situation? Describe one situation in your life where you need to start making a declaration of faith.

> *There will be people, betrayals, delays, and all kinds of situations that can cause you to live sour.*

....

....

....

....

....

....

....

....

4. What are you telling your feelings when you declare "I will rejoice"? Would you say that your feelings rule over your will most of the time, or vice versa? Explain your answer.

....

....

....

....

....

....

5. Describe an area of your life where you are putting off your happiness until something changes or improves. Why doesn't that ever work?

....

....

....

....

....

6. Why is it true that if you don't get happy where you are, you probably won't get to where you want to be? What is the seed that God uses to change things? Describe a situation where you got stuck until you changed your perspective about it.

....

....

....

....

....

> *You're as happy as you want to be.*

7. What message from the story of the basketball player who was battling cancer do you feel God is speaking to your heart about? Do you see yourself keeping your joy in situations such as that?

....

....

....

....

....

....

8. The psalmist says, "Happy are the people whose God is the LORD" (Ps. 144:15 NKJV). What does this tell you about who God is and what He has ordained for you?

....

....

....

....

....

....

....

9. Why is it significant that David started off by saying, "This is the day the Lord has made"? What was he saying about "this day"? What responsibility do we have in living out "this day"?

....

....

....

....

....

10. Name a few past disappointments, bad breaks, or losses that soured you, that stole your joy. How could you have kept from getting sour and losing your passion in those times?

....

....

....

....

....

11. Psalm 57:7–9 says, "I will sing and make music. Awake, my soul! Awake, harp and lyre! I will awaken the dawn. I will praise you, Lord, among the nations." How might your day be different if you start with a song of praise every morning?

....

....

....

....

....

....

12. What lesson on happiness can you take from the birds? How does that correlate with what the apostle Paul says in Philippians 4:8 and what you think about?

....

....

....

....

....

....

> *You can't take in the negative all the time and stay in faith.*

13. From 2 Corinthians 11:23–28, detail some of the difficulties Paul endured while on his missionary journeys. How does his list compare with your difficulties?

....

....

....

....

14. Despite everything that Paul went through, when he was brought out of prison to defend himself before King Agrippa, the first thing he said was, "I think myself happy, King Agrippa, because today I shall answer for myself before you" (Acts 26:2 NKJV). How did he not see himself as a victim? What does that tell you about the power of your thoughts?

....

....

....

....

....

....

....

15. We all face hurts, disappointments, and difficulties. How can happy thoughts keep you from becoming angry and bitter? Write out some happy thoughts that you can use to defeat whatever is worrying or stressing you out, whatever regularly sours your day.

....

....

....

....

....

....

16. Despite Paul's great speech to King Agrippa and his thinking himself happy, he went back to prison and eventually ended up in a prison in Rome. Write down what Paul told the Philippians to do while he was in prison (Phil. 4:4). What valuable lesson can you take from Paul's experience?

....

....

....

....

....

....

17. Do you actually believe in your heart that God wants you to be happy? Have you given yourself permission to be happy? Write a prayer to the Lord, telling Him how you feel as you reflect on your happiness and asking Him to help you hear what He's saying to you.

....

....

....

....

....

....

18. Paul says, "Be happy in your faith and rejoice and be glad-hearted continually" (1 Thess. 5:16 AMPC). Why didn't he mention anything about our circumstances? How can you stop negative circumstances from talking you out of living happy?

Are you thinking yourself sad, thinking yourself discouraged, thinking yourself a victim?

....

....

....

....

....

19. Read Habakkuk 3:17–18. How does the prophet's situation and his attitude toward it strengthen your faith and resolve as you see darkness and uncertainty in the world around you?

....

....

....

....

....

....

20. What was your immediate response to the statement that "believers should be the happiest people on earth"? Would you say that people see the joy in you?

....

....

....

....

....

21. When you think about the best day of your life, what day would it be? As good as that was, how is it possible to make this day, every day, your best day?

....

....

....

....

....

22. James asks the question, "For what is your life? It is even a vapor that appears for a little time and then vanishes away" (James 4:14 NKJV). How valuable does that make today? What are some things you can do today to make the very most of it? What did the young mother who was dying of cancer do?

....

....

....

....

....

....

23. When the apostle Paul came to the end of his life, he said that he only wanted to "finish my course with joy" (Acts 20:24 AMPC). Write a prayer that expresses the desire of your heart to live full of joy right up until the last day of your life.

....

....

....

....

....

....

CHAPTER FOUR

Let Go of Control

God puts promises and dreams in our hearts. We know we're going to get well, we know our business is going to succeed, we know we're going to meet the right person. But God doesn't tell us how or when it's going to happen. Too often if it's not happening the way we thought or on our timetable, we get frustrated. "God, when is this going to turn around? When is my health going to improve? Why isn't this situation at work getting better?"

1. When a situation isn't working out, most of us try to put God in a box and tell Him how to do it, when it should happen, and who to use. Would you say that describes what you do? Write a typical example from your experience and what the usual outcome is.

....
....
....
....
....

2. Once you pray about a situation that's not changing, once you believe, what do you have to do? What happens when you try to control the outcome?

....
....
....
....
....

3. Take some time and think about what's upsetting you right now. What's keeping you awake at night? What is God saying to you about it?

....

....

....

....

....

....

4. The Scripture says, "We who have believed enter that rest" (Heb. 4:3). The rest of faith is a place of peace. In what ways would you like more peace and rest in your life?

....

....

....

....

....

....

5. Write a prayer to the Lord, telling Him what you want to rest in faith about and releasing the worries, the frustrations, and the discouragements that you are feeling.

You can't trust God and be worried at the same time.

....

....

....

....

....

....

6. There are times when we want something so badly, it can get out of balance. What is the danger in doing that? Describe a time when you let your desires or your dream to become too strong. What was the outcome?

....

....

....

Hold tightly to your dreams, but hold loosely to how God is going to do it.

....

....

....

7. What do you need to do when you realize that what you want has gotten out of balance? Have you seen God do things in unusual, unexpected ways in your life? Describe what happened.

....

....

....

....

....

....

....

8. Looking back, have you experienced a time when you were upset about something that you later realized was the hand of God at work? What lesson can you take from that situation?

....

....

....

....

....

9. Describe some of the detours, curves, delays, and times when you felt as though you were going the wrong way. How did you respond to those times? What happens when you get set on the method for how things work out?

....

....

....

....

....

10. Read Psalm 102:13. If there are set times of favor for your life, what does that mean in practical terms for what you're waiting and believing for? Name one situation that you need to believe has a set time on it.

....

....

....

....

....

....

11. What are you passionate about—your dreams, being healed, finding freedom, getting a promotion? How do you keep that from consuming your happiness in the present?

....

....

....

....

....

....

12. Read Joseph's story in Genesis 37. How does his story contradict what we usually think about troubles and setbacks?

....

....

....

....

....

13. Joseph had a God-given dream and knew God's favor was on him, yet what happened to him? Put yourself in his shoes and describe what you would have had to understand and do in order to make it through thirteen years of struggle.

Are you frustrated because you don't understand something that's happened to you?

....

....

....

....

....

14. The Scripture says, "Since the Lord is directing our steps, why try to understand everything that happens along the way?" (Prov. 20:24 TLB). What powerful lesson can you take from this verse and from studying Joseph's journey?

....

....

....

....

....

15. When the soldiers came to arrest Jesus on the Mount of Olives and His disciples were about to pull out their swords, why did Jesus say, "Don't resist anymore" (Luke 22:51 TLB)? As bad as the circumstances looked, what did Jesus understand about what was ahead?

....

....

....

....

....

16. It may have looked as though the enemy was in control when Jesus was taken away, but what was actually happening? What vital truth do you need to remember when you face hardships, bad breaks, and disappointments, and you want to fight and resist?

....

....

....

....

....

17. Jesus faced Judas's kiss. David faced Saul's jealousy. Joseph faced Potiphar's wife's false accusation. The three Hebrew teenagers faced the king's fiery furnace. And they all won. How did they win, and how will you win in difficult situations that you can't control?

....

....

....

....

....

....

18. Even when you've been faithfully doing the right thing for a long time, what looks like the wrong thing can happen and leave you disappointed, even devastated. In these times, you have to be mature enough to know when to resist and when not to resist. Describe a time when you resisted but later realized you should not have. What was the outcome?

> *You're not supposed to fight every battle.*

....

....

....

....

....

....

19. Read Acts 27. Why did they lower the sail and "let the wind carry the ship" (v. 15 CEV)? What does that tell you to do when you've done everything you can but it's not working?

....

....

....

....

....

....

20. When Joseph told his brothers, whose actions led to thirteen years of trouble for him, that "you intended to harm me, but God intended it for good" (Gen. 50:20), what was he saying to us about times when we're trying to control things and force them to go our way?

....

....

....

....

....

....

21. What valuable lesson can you take from the lady who got tuberculosis, lost her job and her apartment and her truck? How did the winds of the storm blow her to where God wanted her to be?

....

....

....

....

....

22. When you're tempted to think that a difficulty or trouble is going to stop you, what truth about God will keep your faith strong?

....

....

....

....

....

23. Psalm 55:22 AMPC says, "Cast your burden on the Lord [releasing the weight of it] and He will sustain you." Don't end this chapter carrying around a weight of worry, of what you don't understand, of how you're not going to make it through a tough season. No matter what it is, write a prayer to the Lord and release it into His hands and enter into His rest.

....

....

....

....

....

....

CHAPTER FIVE

Unclutter Your Mind

It's easy to be worried about our future, stressed over our finances, frustrated with our boss. We're tempted to live feeling guilty about past mistakes, bitter over what failed, upset about the person who did us wrong. We wonder why we can't sleep at night, why we don't enjoy our life, why we're not passionate about our dreams. It's because our mind is cluttered. You can't stop negative things from coming, but you can keep them from staying.

1. Would you describe your mind as a cluttered mind? Do you hold on to mistakes, worry and stress, guilt and condemnation, and go around being down on yourself? Write an honest review.

   ....

   ....

   ....

   ....

   ....

2. Philippians 4:7 says, "And the peace of God, which transcends all understanding, will guard your hearts and your minds in Christ Jesus." How do you guard your mind from the noise, drama, stress, worry, guilt, and jealousy that come against you today?

   ....

   ....

   ....

   ....

   ....

3. What valuable lesson can you take from the lady who was a hoarder? Whether she was aware of it or not, what was she doing to her life?

> *Living cluttered had become normal to her.*

....

....

....

....

....

....

4. Would you say that you are a hoarder in your mind? Describe one area of your thoughts where you need an intervention.

....

....

....

....

....

....

....

5. Sometimes we've been living worried, living guilty, or living inferior for so many years that it's become normal to us. Take some time to think about where that may be true for you. How do you clean out that clutter?

....

....

....

....

....

....

....

....

6. What have you already experienced as consequences from the clutter in your mind?

....

....

....

....

....

7. When you have held on to hurts in the past, was it worth it? Did it lead to anything good? Did your reasons for holding on make sense?

....

....

....

....

....

8. How much emotional energy do you waste every day on grudges and hurts? Where should that energy be directed? How does God give you "beauty for ashes" (Isa. 61:3 NKJV)?

....

....

....

....

....

9. Describe a time when you made the mistake of trying to get even with someone. What was the outcome?

....

....

....

....

....

10. Read Psalm 23:5. Rather than try to pay people back, how can God vindicate you better than you can vindicate yourself? How did the acquisition of the Compaq Center demonstrate that?

....

....

....

....

....

11. When you have opposition, when you have trouble, when people come against you, what is the key thing to do? Write out Psalm 46:10 and begin to commit it to memory.

> *When you're at peace, that's a position of power.*

....

....

....

....

....

12. Read the amazing story in 2 Chronicles 20:1–29. When God says to "stand still," what does He mean? Describe a time when He said it to you. What was the outcome?

....

....

....

....

....

....

....

13. What is the enemy's main target? Why?

....

....

....

14. Read 2 Chronicles 32:1–23. What was King Hezekiah's initial response when it was clear that Jerusalem was the next city in line to be attacked by the Assyrians?

....

....

....

....

....

15. When you are facing a big enemy, what is the first thing you have to remind yourself of?

....

....

....

....

16. What did the king of Assyria try to do in preparation for the attack upon Israel? What did he say? What has the enemy said to you to set you up for defeat?

....

....

....

....

....

....

17. What did King Hezekiah and the prophet Isaiah do together? What happened as a result? What lesson can you take from them?

....

....

....

....

....

18. There are some things we can't fix. Describe a time when you tried to do what only God can do. What was the result? Looking back, what should you have done?

Our part is to believe, our part is to stay in faith, and then let God do His part.

....

....

....

....

....

....

....

....

19. The prophet Isaiah says, "You will keep him in perfect peace, whose mind is stayed on You, because he trusts in You" (Isa. 26:3 NKJV). Describe a situation that you couldn't fix, but you stayed in faith and waited. What was the outcome?

....

....

....

....

....

....

....

20. Read Daniel 3. Describe the attitude of faith demonstrated by the three Hebrew teenagers. What was the powerful key to their position? How does that take away the enemy's power?

....

....

....

....

....

21. Write a declaration of faith similar to the three Hebrew teenagers' declaration that speaks to a situation in your life that is not changing or not going your way.

....

....

....

....

....

22. Do you pay attention to all the negative things that you're allowing into your spirit? How can you keep from repeating the same painful mistakes?

....

....

....

....

23. Are you hooked on drama and living on the edge, full of worry and frustration, or are you believing that God created you to live from a place of peace? What change in your thinking will help you improve in this area?

....

....

....

....

....

24. If you're going to give birth to your potential, what lesson can you take from ewes when it comes to lambing? How do you live out of a quiet place when there's noise all around?

> *An uncluttered mind is a powerful force.*

25. David's life was filled with constant challenges and difficulties, yet he says, "He makes me lie down in green pastures, he leads me besides quiet waters, he refreshes my soul" (Ps. 23:2–3). What is God saying to you through these verses? What has He been saying to you throughout this chapter? Write a summary of His thoughts toward you.

CHAPTER SIX

Dealing with Difficult People

I thought about titling this chapter "Dealing with Friends, Family, and Coworkers." There's someone at work who has a way of getting on your nerves, or a friend who gets jealous and gives you the silent treatment, or a child who is really difficult. It might be a neighbor who's rude or a relative who's not for you and talks about you. How you handle difficult people will determine how high you will go.

1. The apostle Paul says, "Do not be overcome by evil, but overcome evil with good" (Rom. 12:21). What was your immediate response to that statement? Did it make sense to you? Describes some situations where you overcame evil with good.

....

....

....

....

....

2. Year after year, there are some people or some situations that we all have let upset us. Name a few of yours. Do you believe that you can change and stay in peace?

Why don't you take the controls back?

....

....

....

....

....

3. Jesus says, "Peace I leave with you; My peace I now give you...Stop allowing your-selves to be agitated and disturbed" (John 14:27 AMPC). What buttons do people push that get you bent out of shape? Do you believe that someone can make you get upset?

....

....

....

....

....

4. What are some practical ways that you can stay on the high road when they push your buttons? What statements can you have ready to empower you to stay on the offensive?

....

....

....

....

....

5. The Scripture says, "If your enemy is hungry, feed him; if he is thirsty, give him some-thing to drink. In doing this, you will heap burning coals on his head" (Rom. 12:20). What does it mean to "heap burning coals" on someone? What are some ways that you can be good to someone who is not good to you?

....

....

....

....

....

6. The prophet Isaiah says, "Those who hope in the LORD will renew their strength. They will soar on wings like eagles" (Isa. 40:31). Why did God choose to refer to believers as eagles? What does that tell you about the life God created you to live?

....

....

....

....

....

....

7. What lesson can you take from the relationship between eagles and crows? What is the best way to deal with the people who make it their purpose to annoy and irritate you?

....

....

....

....

....

8. What can't you stop about the crows, the chickens, and the turkeys in your life? How do you not let them become a distraction?

> *God put greatness in you.*

....

....

....

....

....

....

9. Negative chatter can come at you from so many ways today, especially social media. What way do you find the most troublesome? How do you keep from giving your power away in your responses to other people's critical opinions about you?

....

....

....

....

....

....

10. Read 2 Kings 2. Describe what had happened to Elisha just before his encounter with the disrespectful young men. How might Elisha have responded versus how he did respond? What does that tell you about God being your vindicator when you face disrespect and jealousy?

....

....

....

....

....

....

11. Psalm 45:7 ESV says, "God, your God, has anointed you with the oil of gladness beyond your companions." When you walk in your anointing, how are you like a Teflon pan? Name some specific ways.

....

....

....

....

....

....

12. In Chapter Three, we established that we control our own happiness. Describe a recent situation where you let someone steal your joy. How would you handle your response differently if it came up today?

....

....

....

....

....

....

13. The parts clerk in the electronics store was extremely offensive and bad-mannered. Have you ever encountered someone like him who was that offensive toward you? How did you respond? What was the outcome?

> *You have to make up your mind that no matter what people say or how they treat you, they're not going to steal your joy.*

....

....

....

....

....

14. How do you keep other people's poison from getting in you when they start dumping their trash on you?

....

....

....

....

....

....

15. People will steal our joy if we have unrealistic expectations of them, such as that they should never be rude but always say nice things about us. What are some of the unrealistic expectations you have of others that easily get you upset?

....

....

....

....

....

....

16. Describe a recent situation where you had a made-up mind to not let someone's negative comments or behavior toward you to sour your day. How can you make deciding ahead of time a priority every day?

....

....

....

....

....

....

17. It's hard to not take someone's rudeness personally. To keep it from becoming personal, what do you need to remind yourself is going on inside that person?

....

....

....

....

....

....

18. Read 1 Samuel 25. Describe the background between David and Nabal as well as the character of Nabal. Was David's request reasonable?

....

....

....

....

19. Was David's vindictive response to Nabal's rudeness justifiable? What mistake did David make that could have hindered his destiny? What lesson can you take from his mistake?

....

....

....

....

....

....

20. What wisdom did Abigail bring to David that calmed him down? How did she take the personal sting out of the insult and put the situation in the right perspective?

....

....

....

....

....

21. What questions do you need to ask yourself the next time you encounter a Nabal?

....

....

....

....

....

22. How does the relationship of Abigail and David reflect what happens when you let God fight your battles rather than try to pay back others for their offenses?

....

....

....

....

....

....

....

....

....

23. Based upon what you've learned in this chapter, what new perspective are you taking from now on when it comes to dealing with difficult people? What changes in your thinking will help you stay in peace and rise above the conflict?

....

....

> *You can't get away from the Nabals. You may pray one away, but Nabal Jr. will show up tomorrow.*

....

....

....

....

....

....

....

CHAPTER SEVEN

Live in the Present

So often our mind is either in the past, focused on what didn't work out, who did us wrong, mistakes we've made, or it's in the future, thinking about our goals, worried about our finances, worried about our health. The problem with being in the past or being in the future is that you will miss the present.

1. David says, "This is the day that the LORD has made; let us rejoice and be glad in it" (Ps. 118:24 ESV). What is he saying about today? Would you say that you tend to spend more time in yesterday or in tomorrow than being fully engaged in the present, making the most of each moment? Explain your answer.

....

....

....

....

....

2. What does it mean to "show up for life"? How do you balance that with focusing on your goals and vision?

....

....

....

....

....

....

....

3. Describe a time when you were either so focused on the past or the future that you missed what should have been a special time in the present. If you could go back in time, what would you tell yourself?

....

....

....

....

....

....

4. Who would you say are the most valuable people in your life? Are you living in the present with them, or are you missing out? Are you taking them for granted?

> *The people in your life are not always going to be there.*

....

....

....

....

....

....

5. What are some ways that you can start to make the most of the moments with your family and loved ones? What reminders can help keep you present and connected?

....

....

....

....

....

....

6. It's easy to go on autopilot with our spouse or another loved one. Do you find yourself just going through the motions? What do you need to do to get plugged back in?

....
....
....
....
....

7. The Scripture says, "For this reason a man will leave his father and mother and be united to his wife, and the two will become one flesh" (Matt. 19:5). What does "becoming one" say about a marital relationship? What do we have to realize about each other over the years?

....
....
....
....
....

8. What does it mean that a couple can "live in the house, but they're really not home. They sleep in the same bed, but they're not there"? What can change that at this very moment?

....
....
....
....
....
....

Give that person room to be human.

9. The danger of living disconnected as a couple is that it can lead to a breakup of the relationship. What indicators show that this is happening, and what do you need to remember about the sacredness of what God has given you?

....

....

....

....

....

....

....

10. Laughter is like medicine within a family. What ways have you found to keep your family laughing together, having fun together? Are there some new things you can do to make your home a place of joy?

....

....

....

....

....

....

....

11. Living in strife and holding grudges will keep you from the new things God has in store. How do you keep them out of your family relationships?

....

....

....

....

....

....

12. In Chapter Four, you read the beginning of Joseph's story in Genesis 37. Now read Genesis 39–40. Describe the difficulties that Joseph went through that could have easily kept him living in the past. What must that have felt like?

....

....

....

....

....

....

13. How could Joseph keep such a good attitude after all he went through? What thoughts helped keep his spirit so excellent in the darkness of that prison?

It takes maturity to enjoy where you are even though you have challenges.

....

....

....

....

....

....

14. Life is not about the destination; it's about the journey. What does this life principle tell you about the times when problems are not turning around and the dream seems impossible?

....

....

....

....

....

15. Read Genesis 41. What does this chapter tell you about the promises of God? What does it tell you about Joseph's past years of discouragement, worry, and loneliness?

....

....

....

....

....

....

16. Are you waiting for a promise of God to come to pass? What is it? How are you spending the time while you're waiting? What is the key to staying in faith?

....

....

....

....

....

....

17. Describe a time when you kept believing that God was ordering your steps despite all the odds being against you. What was the outcome?

....

....

....

....

....

....

18. What valuable lesson can you take away from the story of the executive who was unexpectedly let go from her company? How could she have easily chosen to live in the past or in the future? What would she have missed?

> *Trust God enough to enjoy your life.*

....

....

....

....

....

....

19. Rather than embracing where you are today, are you fighting where you are, fighting something that's not working out and you don't understand? What change in your thinking will help you not miss the beauty of this day?

....

....

....

....

....

....

20. Ephesians 5:16 VOICE says, "Make the most of every living and breathing moment because these are evil times." Start to commit this verse to memory and make it a life principle you embrace. Write a declaration of your bold commitment to living in the present.

....

....

....

....

....

....

....

21. All through the day, it's good to take a few deep breaths and just breathe in God's goodness, to enjoy God in the present. How can you start to make this a part of every day?

....

....

....

....

....

....

22. Did the pandemic or another time when something in your life was taken away and then given back change your perspective on what you have? What changed?

....

....

....

....

....

....

23. Based on what you have learned in this chapter, take a moment and reflect on how you can start living every day to the full.

....

....

....

....

....

....

CHAPTER EIGHT

Let It Go

We all go through disappointments, things that are not fair. It's easy to hold on to the hurts, to think about what they said, to relive the offense. We get up in the morning and it's the first thing that comes to mind. We don't realize how much that's affecting us. It's souring our attitude, draining our energy, and limiting our creativity. If you're going to fulfill your destiny, you have to get good at letting things go.

1. Jesus says, "Offenses will certainly come" (Luke 17:1 CSB). Describe a time when a major offense came your way. How did you handle that offense? What was the outcome?

   ....

   ....

   ....

   ....

   ....

   ....

2. Why is it true that until you stop carrying a hurt, until you let go of what didn't work out, that wound is going to hinder you wherever you go? In what ways have you experienced this?

   ....

   ....

   ....

   ....

   ....

   ....

   ....

3. After someone has hurt you, what happens to you if you hold on to it? Describe a time when you let that happen to you. How did it impact you?

> *You have to heal so you can see new relationships and opportunities.*

....

....

....

....

....

....

....

4. When Peter asked Jesus how many times he should forgive someone, Jesus answered, "I do not say to you, up to seven times, but up to seventy times seven" (Matt. 18:22 NKJV). What principle was Jesus stating here?

....

....

....

....

....

....

....

5. What did Jesus specifically tell us to pray in Matthew 6:12? What qualifies as a "trespass against us" or as a "debtor"? Did He say there are exceptions, whether big or small?

....

....

....

....

....

....

6. Read 1 Samuel 16:1–13. How was David treated by his own father? Have you ever been treated that way by someone? Describe how you responded to one of those incidents.

....

....

....

....

....

....

7. Read 1 Samuel 17:28–29. How was David treated by his oldest brother? Have you ever been treated that way? Describe how you responded to one of those incidents.

....

....

....

....

....

8. Having considered how unfair David was treated, is there some offense that you're holding on to that is causing you to be sour? How do you get past the offense and move forward to a new level?

....

....

....

....

....

....

9. Read 1 Samuel 17:40–54. What did God do for David after he had let go of the offenses of his father and brother? What lesson can you take from that?

> *God saw what happened to you in the past, so let it go.*

....

....

....

....

....

....

10. What message of hope do you take from the story of the young man whose father left the family and later refused to see him? Do you know anyone who has gone through something similar? Did that person come out as this man did, rising higher and seeing God's goodness?

....

....

....

....

....

....

....

11. What happens when you bury or bottle up negative emotions? Why does that make forgiveness so important?

....

....

....

....

....

12. Have you ever experienced anything even close to the anger and hostility that the professional boxer had toward his father? Describe your experience.

....
....
....
....
....
....

13. Both the one young man and the boxer grew up in very similar situations. What was the difference between how the abuse and abandonment effected them? How does one see beauty out of the ashes?

....
....
....
....
....
....

14. In what ways was the toxic waste site similar to what happens when we bury bitterness, hatred, and rejection? What is the only solution to contaminations such as these?

....
....
....
....
....
....

15. Read 1 Samuel 19:1–12. How was David treated by King Saul? Have you ever tried to be helpful and kind to someone who later treated you badly? Describe how you responded. Did your response lead to an improved relationship?

....

....

....

....

....

16. Read 2 Samuel 1:17–27. If someone treated you as Saul did David, putting your life at risk for years, can you imagine writing a song of lamentation over them, calling them "beloved and gracious"? What would you have written? How is it possible that David carried no bitterness toward Saul?

It's not always easy to forgive, but it's harder to deal with the poison of unforgiveness.

....

....

....

....

....

17. What valuable lesson can you take from the experience of Rudy Tomjanovich? Why were people so shocked by his response to the person who nearly killed him?

....

....

....

....

....

18. Have you ever done as Tomjanovich did and forgiven someone who hurt you before the toxins could get inside, forgiven so that you could be free? Describe what happened.

....

....

....

....

....

....

19. Read 2 Samuel 12:1–23. As with David, there are times when our own sins and failures lead to a great deal of pain and damage. What does David show us about the path to recovery when we face despair, shame, and condemnation over what we've done?

....

....

....

....

....

....

....

20. Read 2 Samuel 12:24–25. Had David stayed in a state of grief and disappointment, what would have happened? What is its message of hope for you today and in the future?

....

....

....

....

....

....

....

21. How does the story of the eagle and the mole describe what too often happens in our life?

....

....

....

....

....

22. Are you holding on to something that you don't realize is killing you? If there's anger, bitterness, guilt, or shame, that's draining the life out of you. Before you close this chapter, you can be free. From what you've learned in this chapter, write a statement declaring that you are forgiving and letting go of whatever is holding you back, that you're releasing any toxins that have been buried, and you're going to live in freedom from now on.

....

....

....

....

Today can be a turning point.

....

....

....

....

....

....

....

....

CHAPTER NINE

Nothing to Prove

Too often we're trying to get our worth from what we do. So much of it is about how well we think we're performing. We ask ourself, "Am I a good enough parent? Am I talented enough, strong enough, successful enough?" We think if we work harder, outperform our coworker, outdress our friend, or outdrive our neighbor, we'll feel good about ourself. We live in a proving mode with this need to impress.

1. What is the problem with living in a proving mode? In what ways have you struggled with trying to gain other people's approval? Are these still a struggle for you?

....
....
....
....
....
....

2. What is the key to finding freedom from living in the proving mode? Have you recognized that this is true in your life? In what ways do you, and in what ways have you not?

....
....
....
....
....
....

3. What lesson can you take from the man whose father told him that he would never amount to anything? Have you experienced anything similar to that? How has it impacted you?

> *Do you think you will feel good about yourself when you get successful or strong enough?*

....

....

....

....

....

....

4. Do you have someone who you're trying to prove that you're as good as them? What change in your thinking will keep you from living with this frustration?

....

....

....

....

....

5. What does it mean that "you are competing in a race that was never designed for you"? Have you recognized who God made you to be and the power of believing that?

....

....

....

....

....

....

6. Hebrews 12:1 says, "Let us run with perseverance the race marked out for us." What does that mean when you find yourself comparing yourself with others? Name some specific ways that you've had to hold to your race rather than compete.

....

....

....

....

....

....

....

7. Do you struggle with thoughts that if you read your Bible enough, pray enough, quote enough Scripture, serve enough, and give enough that you'll be good enough? Search out and write down some Scriptures that counter these thoughts and arm yourself with them.

....

....

....

....

....

....

....

8. Read Galatians 1:10. What did the apostle Paul state was the problem with trying to impress people and win their approval? Whose approval is all we need?

....

....

....

....

....

....

9. Read Romans 12:3–8. In what ways has God gifted you? How should the knowledge of your gifting defeat feelings of inferiority? Has it for you? In what ways has it not?

....

....

....

....

....

....

10. What lesson can you take from the man who kept driving past his ex-girlfriend's house? Have you ever found yourself doing something similar? Explain your answer.

....

....

....

....

....

....

11. Is there one major thing that you think would increase your self-worth if you could just change it? Why is that a dead-end street?

How much energy are you spending trying to feel good enough, talented enough, smart enough, worthy enough?

....

....

....

....

....

12. Read Luke 3:21–22. What is so interesting about what God the Father said about Jesus at His baptism? Do you believe He says the same about you? Knowing this, how do you feel?

....

....

....

....

....

....

13. Numbers 6:24–25 MSG says, "GOD bless you and keep you, GOD smile upon you." Do you believe that God smiles on you? Even if you feel you don't measure up? What is God showing us about Himself, and how does that impact our relationships with other people?

....

....

....

....

....

14. Write a prayer to the Lord, telling Him how you feel as you reflect on what it means to know that He is pleased with you and that He smiles upon you.

....

....

....

....

....

....

15. Read Luke 4:1–13. Describe a time when you felt that God led you into the wilderness. How did you respond? What was the outcome?

Keep in mind that you can be in the desert by God's design.

16. What test did Jesus have to pass in the wilderness temptations? What was His response?

17. What powerful lesson can you take away from Jesus' example here?

18. Jesus has all-power and could have used it to prove who He was, but He refused. You may have the power to prove something—you have the talent and the funds. You could get even, you could show off, you could impress, but why is that a waste of time and energy? What should you be doing instead?

....

....

....

....

....

....

19. The enemy tried three times to get Jesus to prove Himself. What does that tell you about getting into the proving mode? Have you recognized that it is true in your life? How so?

....

....

....

....

....

....

20. When you're tempted to start to compete and prove yourself to others, why is it so important to consider your motives? What questions can you ask yourself to keep from falling into the wrong motives?

....

....

....

....

....

....

21. Read 1 Samuel 17. What was David's motive when he went out to face Goliath? What lesson can you take from David's example?

....
....
....
....
....

David's brother and father as well as King Saul didn't believe in him.

....
....
....
....

22. After studying this chapter, what new perspective are you taking from now on about trying to prove yourself? Write a summary of what you've learned.

....
....
....
....
....
....
....
....
....
....
....

CHAPTER TEN

Don't Rely on People

It's great when people believe in us, cheer us on, and make us feel valuable. We love when our spouse, a friend, or a coworker gives a compliment or an encouragement. God uses people to help move us toward our destiny. But here's the key: You can't become so dependent on people that you're getting your worth and value from how they treat you.

1. To what degree would you say that you rely on other people to keep you feeling good about yourself? Take some time to reflect on this and write an honest review.

> It's easy to become addicted to others making you feel approved.

....

....

....

....

....

....

2. Read John 18:15–27. What did Jesus show us about relying on people, even the closest people, and when you need them the most?

....

....

....

....

....

....

....

3. If you depend on somebody else for approval, you'll become needy, always waiting for other people to keep you fixed. On a scale of 1 to 10, with 1 being needy, and 10 being happy and content with God's approval, how would you grade yourself? Explain your answer.

    ....

    ....

    ....

    ....

    ....

    ....

    ....

4. If you haven't gotten what you think you should have from someone, what do you need to understand about it?

    ....

    ....

    ....

    ....

    ....

5. Jesus said to His religious critics, "Your approval or disapproval means nothing to me" (John 5:41 TLB). What lesson can you take from Jesus' example?

    ....

    ....

    ....

    ....

    ....

    ....

6. The apostle Paul said, "I am self-sufficient in Christ's sufficiency" (Phil. 4:13 AMPC). What does that mean? What does that have to do with living approved?

....

....

....

....

....

....

7. Psalm 75:6 TLB says, "For promotion and power come from nowhere on earth, but only from God." What message does this tell you in times when you are trying to convince someone to make a connection for you or advance you? How do you feel knowing that?

....

....

....

....

....

You have the applause from the One who matters most.

8. What is the reason that some people don't give us what we need? When you realize this is true of someone you know, how should it change your expectations?

....

....

....

....

....

....

9. You have to learn to build yourself up, to encourage yourself, to compliment yourself. What does God say about you that you can use to start building yourself up? Write it down and begin to speak it out loud.

    ....

    ....

    ....

    ....

    ....

    ....

10. Take some time and recognize some of the people whom you've relied upon to meet your needs and you realized it was too much. Describe what was involved.

    ....

    ....

    ....

    ....

    ....

    ....

11. What was your immediate response to the statement "Nobody owes me anything"? Do you believe that no one owes you anything? What freedom is found in it?

    ....

    ....

    ....

    ....

    ....

    ....

12. Is there someone who failed to meet a need of yours in the past that you realize you need to let off the hook? Describe what happened and then write a declaration that you are letting go of it and that they owe you nothing.

....

....

....

....

....

....

13. Can someone make you whole again after they've hurt you? Have you tried to get somebody to apologize, to admit they were wrong? Describe it. What was the outcome?

....

....

....

....

....

....

14. God has seen every negative thing that's happened to you. What can He do for you that only He can do?

God is keeping all the records.

....

....

....

....

....

....

15. Describe one of your closest relationships in the context of the 80/20 percent principle. What makes up the 20 percent that you're missing as well as the other person's 20 percent?

....

....

....

....

....

....

16. What is the key to a good relationship? Describe what is best about one of your good relationships.

....

....

....

....

....

....

17. How has God used compliments and encouragement from others in a positive way in your life? Name some specific examples.

....

....

....

....

....

....

18. Sometimes God will let us go through seasons where we're not getting what we expect from people. Describe a time in your life when He purposefully weaned you off others' approval and validation. How did you feel going through that?

....
....
....
....
....
....
....

19. During that season of your life, how was God growing you up? In what ways did you discover that you needed to change?

....
....
....
....
....
....
....

20. When you come to the end of life, what is God going to ask you? How does that change your perspective on trying to please people?

....
....
....
....
....
....

21. Read Judges 7. What did God tell Gideon to do with the men who had gathered for war, and why did He tell him that? Put yourself in Gideon's shoes and imagine what he must have been thinking. What lesson can you take from Gideon's experience?

....

....

....

....

....

....

....

....

22. What goal do you want to accomplish or obstacle do you want to overcome that you think you must first have other people to support you? Based upon what you've learned in this chapter, write a declaration that your sufficiency is in Christ's sufficiency and that you are not relying upon others to make it happen.

The less you depend on people, the greater the anointing on your life.

....

....

....

....

....

....

....

....

....

CHAPTER ELEVEN

Be Comfortable Not Knowing

We all have situations that we don't see how they're going to work out. We study the facts, the numbers, the reports, and the odds are against us. We do our best to come up with a plan, to find a solution. We think we have to have the answer or it's not going to happen. But there are some things that God doesn't want us to know. He has the solution, but if He showed you right now, it wouldn't take any faith.

1. What was your first thought when you read the statement "You have to be comfortable not knowing"? Describe a situation that you are facing right now for which you have no solution despite trying everything you can think. How "comfortable" are you feeling about it?

   ....

   ....

   ....

   ....

2. Read Exodus 13:21–22. Other than the pillar of cloud and pillar of fire to guide them, what answers could Moses give the two million Israelites who asked what route they were taking to the Promised Land, where the food and water was coming from, or how they would be protected? What did Moses have to do, and what did the Israelites have to do?

   Just because you don't know doesn't mean God doesn't have a plan.

   ....

   ....

   ....

   ....

3. Psalm 139:16 NCV says, "All the days planned for me were written in your book before I was one day old." God has a blueprint for your life, but what is the catch? Why doesn't He just show everything that's coming right now?

....

....

....

....

....

....

4. What does faith say about some of the biggest challenges you face that you don't see how they're going to turn out?

....

....

....

....

....

....

5. Are you the type of person who obsesses over trying to figure everything out and having a plan? How stressed out do you get when you have no plan? How is being able to say, "I don't know how it's going to work out, but I'm at peace," not a lack of faith?

....

....

....

....

....

....

6. What valuable lessons can you take from the story of the scheduled payments due for the renovation of the Compaq Center?

....

....

....

....

....

7. Moses had no answers to the many questions of how the Israelites would get to the Promised Land, but name some of the miracles that God did for them. What is its message of hope and assurance for answers you don't have today and won't have in the future?

....

....

....

....

....

....

....

8. Proverbs 3:5 says, "Trust in the LORD with all your heart and lean not on your own understanding." In what sense is that saying there are times when you just have to turn your mind off and stop worrying?

....

....

....

....

....

....

....

9. Describe a time when your faith was tested because you had no answers or solutions to a problem that had to be resolved. What was the outcome? What did you learn through that experience that can help keep you from living frustrated today?

....

....

....

....

....

10. The apostle Paul says, "We do not know what we ought to pray for, but the Spirit himself intercedes for us through wordless groans" (Rom. 8:26). Did this admission that "we do not know" represent a lack of faith in this brilliant apostle? How do you feel knowing that?

....

....

....

....

....

11. After Paul writes that "we do not know," what does he write in verse 28 that we do know? How can you start to make this verse your confession of faith that answers doubts and fears when you don't understand or have answers?

> *Don't let what you don't know and what you can't see keep you from releasing your faith.*

....

....

....

....

....

....

12. Read Acts 16:16–40. Describe Paul and Silas's situation. Was there anything fair about what they were subjected to? In a situation that is totally out of your control such as this one, how do you think you would respond? What would you have been thinking?

....
....
....
....
....
....

13. This situation could have led to the death of Paul and Silas. What lesson can you take from their response to it? What was the result, not just for them but for the jailer?

....
....
....
....
....
....

14. Name some situations in your life about which you need to start saying, "I know not… but I know that God…" Why is that so powerful?

....
....
....
....
....
....

15. When you face a challenge and don't see an answer, how can you silence the voice that constantly whispers, "What are you going to do? What are you going to do?"

....

....

....

....

....

....

16. What lesson can you take away from the man who was in a legal battle for ten years? In a situation such as this one, what does it mean to take yourself off the throne and put God back on the throne?

> *God's ways are better than our ways. What He has in mind is much better than what we have in mind.*

....

....

....

....

....

....

....

17. Describe a time when you didn't see an answer to a problem, but God surprised you and made a way where there was no way. What encouragement does this give you for today?

....

....

....

....

....

....

18. Read Genesis 12:1–5. What did Abraham and Sarah have to be comfortable not knowing? Describe situations where some other heroes of the faith said "I know not, but…"

....

....

....

....

....

....

19. Read Genesis 22. Isaac was the son born to Abraham and Sarah based upon the promise of God when they were far too old to have children. How was it possible that God was now asking Abraham to sacrifice Isaac? What can you learn from Abraham's response?

....

....

....

....

....

....

20. How can you use the ram that was way up on the mountain as a daily reminder of how God is your Jehovah Jireh? What is its message of hope and expectancy?

....

....

....

....

....

....

21. Because you trust God when you don't understand, because you're comfortable not knowing, He is going to do things in your life that you can't explain. What is God saying to you that He wants you to keep believing for even though it's been a long time?

....

....

....

> *When you pass the test of not knowing, God has provision coming, things that you couldn't make happen.*

....

....

....

....

....

....

22. What lessons have you learned in this chapter that will help you to see the fulfillment of promises that you thought would never happen, of dreams that you've let go of? Write a declaration of how you will keep hope alive.

....

....

....

....

....

....

....

....

....

....

CHAPTER TWELVE

Win the War Within

There's a battle taking place inside each of us. It's a battle between the flesh and the Spirit. The flesh represents our carnal nature, and it shows out in ways such as jealousy, pride, and compromise. It's the easy way to live. You don't have to be disciplined; you just do whatever you feel like doing. If someone is rude to you, you're rude back to them. If you don't feel like having a good attitude, you go through the day sour.

1. The apostle Paul says, "For if you live by [the flesh's] dictates, you will die" (Rom. 8:13 NLT). How does he describe the flesh? Name some of the ways that you routinely battle with the dictates of the flesh.

    ....

    ....

    ....

    ....

    ....

    ....

2. If you keep giving in to the flesh, Paul says, "You will die." What does that mean? What are some of the ways that you've seen this principle at work in your life?

    ....

    ....

    ....

    ....

    ....

> *When you're tempted to compromise and give in to temptation, there's another option— to walk in the Spirit.*

3. Have you recognized ways in which you are being held back because you keep giving in to the dictates of the flesh? Take some time and reflect on the ways the flesh limits you?

....

....

....

....

....

4. The apostle Paul also says, "For the flesh desires what is contrary to the Spirit, and the Spirit what is contrary to the flesh. They are in conflict with each other, so that you are not to do whatever you want" (Gal. 5:17). What does this say about the nature of this battle? Do you recognize it as a battle that you must fight and win, or do you just do what you feel?

....

....

....

....

....

....

5. Galatians 5:16 says, "Walk by the Spirit, and you will not gratify the desires of the flesh." To dethrone the flesh, what will it take in your life? What choices will you need to make?

....

....

....

....

....

....

....

6. Write down Hebrews 12:11. What makes this such a foundational principle to live by?

....

....

....

....

....

....

7. In what areas of your life do you realize that you need to be more disciplined in order to keep the flesh off the throne? What blessings are you expecting to come when you do?

....

....

....

....

....

....

....

8. The apostle Paul says, "I die daily" (1 Cor. 15:31 NKJV). What did he mean? In what practical ways do you need to start dying daily?

....

....

....

....

....

....

9. Second Corinthians 5:17 NKJV says, "If anyone is in Christ, he is a new creation; old things have passed away; behold, all things have become new." Why then does Paul also tell us, "Put off, concerning your former conduct, the old man which grows corrupt according to the deceitful lusts, and be renewed in the spirit of your mind, and that you put on the new man" (Eph. 4:22–24 NKJV)? Wasn't the old man dead?

> *Lazarus wasn't the only one who came back to life.*

....

....

....

....

....

....

10. How is this principle of putting off the old seen in the life of Peter? How did he lose the war that was going on within?

....

....

....

....

....

....

11. What is the real reason that you can't control your temper or keep your eyes on the right things? What discipline do you need to exercise in order to keep the old man down?

....

....

....

....

....

....

12. What is the meaning of the statement "Anything you defeat quickly is not your real enemy"? When God does not get rid of a temptation or a desire, what does He do? In that case, what do you need to do?

....

....

....

....

....

....

13. Revisit the story of Nabal, Abigail, and David in 1 Samuel 25. How was Nabal symbolic of our old nature?

....

....

....

....

....

....

14. What could never happen for Abigail as long as Nabal was alive? Why is it interesting that Nabal died ten days after Abigail did the right thing and intervened with David?

....

....

....

....

....

....

15. Sometimes a little thing is keeping us from big blessings—a little pride, a little compromise, a little unforgiveness. Just because it seems little doesn't mean it's not a Nabal to us. Name a "little thing" that you need to put down. What do you need to put on instead?

....

....

> *It's time to get rid of Nabal.*

....

....

....

....

16. Read Genesis 27. Describe Jacob's character. Then read Genesis 32:22–32. What changed through Jacob's encounter with God? What changed in you through your encounter with God?

....

....

....

....

....

....

17. After God said that Jacob's name was Israel and he would no longer be called Jacob, why do we read his name as Jacob again and again in Scripture?

....

....

....

....

....

....

18. Describe a recent situation where Jacob showed up in your life when you thought Israel was doing just fine. Who won? Jacob or Israel?

....

....

....

....

....

....

19. Read Genesis 48:1–2. What is so interesting about the use of the names here? Describe a time when you felt as though you were about to give up, that there was no way a situation could work out, but a promise from God suddenly turned it all around.

....

....

....

....

....

....

20. When you wake up in the morning, what choice do you get to make about your day? What difference does it make?

....

....

....

....

....

21. Read Genesis 25:29–34. How does Esau show what can happen when we let carnal desires dictate our actions? How drastic was his loss?

....

....

....

....

....

22. After studying this chapter, would you say that you are winning the war within? Are you walking by the Spirit and not the flesh? Write an honest review. What is the main lesson you have discovered to help you put down the flesh and let the Spirit rule?

....

....

....

> *You can win the war within. God is calling you higher. Whatever you know is holding you back, this is the time to make a change. This is a moment of grace to do what you couldn't do before.*

....

....

....

....

....

....

....

....

CHAPTER THIRTEEN

Tame the Tongue

One reason people get stuck in life is because they haven't learned to control their mouth. They say hurtful things, they put people down, and they argue. They don't realize their mouth is keeping them from rising higher. God won't promote you if you don't have the character to back it up. We have to pay attention to what we're saying. Sometimes our words have been harsh, sarcastic, and condescending for so long that we don't even realize it.

1. The apostle Paul says, "Do not let any unwholesome talk come out of your mouths, but only what is helpful for building others up according to their needs, that it may benefit those who listen" (Eph. 4:29). Would you say that you tend to say everything you feel or that you pause purposefully to consider if what you're about to say will be beneficial to someone?

....

....

....

....

2. What valuable lesson can you take from James 1:19? What are some practical ways you can start to use this in your communications with others?

> *We have two ears and one mouth because we're supposed to listen twice as much as we speak.*

....

....

....

3. Describe a time when you said something in the heat of a battle that you regretted later. What was your thought process in that moment, and what was the outcome? How can you keep from repeating the same painful mistake?

....

....

....

....

....

....

4. What makes the saying, "Sticks and stones may break my bones, but words will never hurt me," so untrue? How is it just the opposite?

....

....

....

....

....

5. David prayed for protection from people who "sharpen their tongues like swords and aim cruel words like deadly arrows" (Ps. 64:3). Describe a time when someone used their words toward you as a sword or an arrow. Have you recovered from the emotional wound?

....

....

....

....

....

....

6. How we speak to our children is a great responsibility. Write a statement that defines how you want to speak to your children, no matter what their age.

....

....

....

....

....

7. What very specific instructions are given to husbands in 1 Peter 3:7? What does this say about the power that a husband has to bless or hurt his wife? Name some examples where you've seen this principle demonstrated in marriage relationships.

Check up on what you're saying. Are you speaking blessings?

....

....

....

....

....

8. Jesus says, "You must give an account on judgment day for every idle word you speak" (Matt. 12:36 NLT). For husbands and wives, what did He mean? Would you say that your words toward your spouse are full of blessing and encouragement?

....

....

....

....

....

9. What are some words of life that you know you need to give to your spouse, or your children, or your friends on a regular basis?

....

....

....

....

....

....

10. Describe a stressful disagreement at your workplace or in your home when you took a step back and didn't say what you felt like saying in that moment. What do you think would have been the result if you had said it?

....

....

....

....

....

....

11. Proverbs 17:9 NLT says, "Love prospers when a fault is forgiven, but dwelling on it separates close friends." Do you have to win and have the last word in arguments? What does love tell you to do instead?

....

....

....

....

....

....

12. Have you experienced how "a ten-minute argument can set a relationship back ten years"? Describe what happened. How does Romans 12:21 speak to situations like these that get heated, disrespectful, and contentious?

....

....

....

....

> *If you argue long enough, you're going to say things that you regret later.*

....

....

13. Proverbs 20:3 NLT says, "Avoiding a fight is a mark of honor; only fools insist on quarreling." Have you thought that avoiding a fight is a mark of honor or a weakness? Explain your thoughts.

....

....

....

....

....

....

14. Do you have someone like Eliab in your life who seems to make it their agenda to bait you into conflict, who knows how to push your buttons? What does it say about your character when you've learned to not answer them but rather turn and walk away?

....

....

....

....

....

....

15. In 1 Peter 3:10 MSG, what does the apostle Peter say is the prescription for loving life and seeing good days? What message do you feel God is speaking to your heart about your words?

....
....
....
....
....

16. Read Psalm 141:1–3. What makes this such a great prayer? Write your own prayer that you can say each morning that asks God to help you take control of what you say. Make a point to declare your prayer boldly every time you're tempted to say things you shouldn't.

....
....
....
....
....
....

17. When Jesus was about to be arrested, He told His disciples, "I will no longer talk much with you, for the ruler of this world is coming" (John 14:30 NKJV). What lesson can you take from His example when you know you're going to be facing a lot of stress and pressure?

....
....
....
....
....
....

18. The apostle Paul says, "If a father dies and leaves an inheritance for his young children, those children are not much better off than slaves until they grow up, even though they actually own everything their father had" (Gal. 4:1 NLT). What does this principle tell you about taming the tongue? What does it have to do with receiving your inheritance?

....

....

....

....

....

19. Read Exodus 14:10–12. What did the Israelites say whenever they got under pressure on the way to the Promised Land? What was the outcome? Do you see a similar pattern in your experience? How do you break it?

> Proverbs says, "Life and death are in the power of the tongue."

....

....

....

....

....

20. In Numbers 12, it says that "the Lord heard" Miriam complaining about Moses and sowing discord with her words. How does what happened to her as a result coincide with the prophet Isaiah's statement that we will eat the fruit of our words?

....

....

....

....

....

....

21. Describe a time when you experienced the power of words in a positive, life-changing way. What was said, and why did it make such an impact for good? What encouragement does this give you about the beneficial power of your words for someone else today?

....

....

....

....

....

....

....

....

....

22. James 3:5–6 NLT says "the tongue is a flame of fire" and that "a tiny spark can set a great forest on fire." The implication here is that one word can start a major problem, but the opposite is also true. One word can start a major blessing. Based upon what you have learned in this chapter, take a moment and reflect on how you can live every day with the intent to start some good fires.

....

....

....

....

....

....

....

....

....

....

....

CHAPTER FOURTEEN

Living Cause-Driven

There should be something we're involved in that's bigger than ourselves. It's good to have personal goals and dreams, things we want to accomplish. But if you're only focused on yourself, you won't reach your highest potential. You were created to help someone else, to be a blessing, to lift the fallen, to encourage those who are down, to fight for those who can't fight for themselves. The next level of your destiny is connected to helping someone else.

1. Do you have a cause that you're passionate about, some way that you can make the world a better place? What is it, and what motivates you to be involved with it? If you don't have a cause, what are your thoughts about finding a cause?

   ....

   ....

   ....

   ....

   ....

2. On a scale of 1 to 10, with 1 being "I only have time to focus on myself," and 10 being "I'm on a mission to help others," how would you grade yourself? What change in your thinking will help you improve in this area?

   ....

   ....

   ....

   ....

   Are you waiting for God to bless you while God is waiting for you to be a blessing?

3. Read 1 Samuel 17:17–24. Why was David's response to his father's request so important? What valuable lesson can you take from it?

....

....

....

....

....

....

4. Read 1 Samuel 17:25–51. What happened when David heard Goliath taunting the Israelite soldiers? When he responded to his brother's criticism and said, "Is there not a cause?" (v. 29 NKJV), what was he saying?

....

....

....

....

....

....

....

5. For David, how was his crown in the cause? How is your crown in your cause?

....

....

....

....

....

....

6. When you have a cause, such as defeating Goliath or acquiring the Compaq Center, what changes in how you believe and pray and live? How has having a cause changed you?

....

....

....

....

....

....

7. David could have been satisfied to live an ordinary life in the shepherds' fields, and you could be satisfied to live an ordinary life doing what you're doing. But God hasn't called you to be ordinary. What has He called you to be? Where do you find that?

....

....

....

....

....

....

> *Where are some giants you can bring down? Where are some people you can lift up?*

8. What makes living comfort-driven attractive to you? What is the problem with that versus living cause-driven? Describe your experience with both.

....

....

....

....

....

....

....

9. You may feel that your cause or a cause you'd like to be involved with is too big for you. What message of encouragement and assurance is found in David's courage?

....

....

....

....

....

10. What valuable lesson can you take from Dr. Price? How did he become the fulfillment of his own prayer?

....

....

....

....

....

11. Isaiah 58:7–8 says, "Is it not to share your food with the hungry and to provide the poor wanderer with shelter—when you see the naked, to cover him…Then your light will break forth like the dawn, and your healing will quickly appear." When you fight for your cause, what will you find?

....

....

....

....

....

....

12. Read Nehemiah 1. Who was Nehemiah, and what did he take up as his cause? What did he not have that was required to fulfill his cause? What did he have?

....

....

....

....

....

....

13. Read Nehemiah 2:1–9. What did Nehemiah ask the king for, and why did he think there was any chance that it would be granted?

....

....

....

....

....

....

14. Is something holding you back from fulfilling your cause? Is there something that you don't have that's required to fulfill it? What do you have?

You don't have to figure it all out. All you have to do is believe.

....

....

....

....

....

....

15. Read Nehemiah 4. After Nehemiah had successfully embarked on his cause, what did he face when he actually began the work on the walls and gates? How did he overcome it?

....

....

....

....

....

....

16. What sort of opposition do you find is the strongest when you step up and fight for your cause? How can you push through it and not be held in check?

....

....

....

....

....

....

17. How long had the walls of Jerusalem been down before Nehemiah made the rebuilding his cause? Who could God have chosen in the decades before? What will the cause bring out in your life?

....

....

....

....

....

....

18. When it comes to fulfilling your dreams or fulfilling your cause, what has to be louder than the loudest naysayers? What have naysayers said to you? How have you responded?

....

....

....

....

....

....

19. Read Luke 22:39–44. Jesus' cause was to give His life on the cross in our behalf and be raised from the dead for our salvation. What did that involve in the garden of Gethsemane when all His emotions said He should give up?

....

....

....

....

....

....

20. When you're in your own garden of Gethsemane, what decision do you have to make in order to fulfill your cause?

....

....

....

....

....

....

21. Read Hebrews 12:1–3. When you grow weary and feel that you're losing heart, how does Jesus show the way ahead? What is His message of hope for you today and in the future?

....
....
....
....
....
....
....
....
....

22. What lessons have you learned in this chapter that will help you live a cause-driven life? Write a declaration of how you will answer the cause and step up to make a difference.

> *When you live cause-driven, your focus is not on how you feel, not on what people are saying, not on what's not working out.*

....
....
....
....
....
....
....
....
....
....

CHAPTER FIFTEEN

Take Care of Yourself

It's easy to get so caught up trying to meet other people's needs and measure up to their expectations that we put ourselves on the back burner. There are the demands at work, pleasing the boss and coworkers. There are family pressures, keeping your spouse happy and caring for your children. There's running to the grocery store and trying to make the perfect dinner that everyone likes. There are friends whom we can't let down.

1. It's easy to develop a hero mentality. Do you feel you always have to be strong, always be the one who comes through, who cheers everyone else up, who fixes the problems? Explain to what level you feel that it is limiting how you care for yourself.

   ....

   ....

   ....

   ....

   ....

2. Would you say that people are making a lot of withdrawals from you, but you're not putting in a lot of deposits? If you're feeling depleted and worn-out, what do you have to do to keep yourself healthy?

   ....

   ....

   ....

   ....

   ....

3. If you are going to live your life in balance, what are some practical changes that you need to make? Take some time to reflect on your daily schedule and commitments.

> *You may have to tell some people that Superman turned back into Clark Kent.*

....
....
....
....
....
....

4. When you've tried to make these adjustments in the past, what stopped you? Did you feel guilty about taking time for yourself or give in to others' expectancies of you? What change in your thinking will help you improve in this area?

....
....
....
....
....
....

5. What do you find that refreshes you, that replenishes you when you feel drained? Have you made that part of your schedule or has it been relegated to rarely happening?

....
....
....
....
....
....

6. Read Luke 5:12–16. Reflect on the never-ending pressures Jesus must have felt to heal and teach and care for others. What does it say to you that He "often withdrew"?

....

....

....

....

....

....

7. If Jesus, the Son of God, had to be alone and rest, if He couldn't meet all the demands of the people around Him, why do most of us think we can go all the time and be everything for everyone? Do you? If His example doesn't convince you to make changes, what will?

....

....

....

....

....

....

....

8. Living drained and depleted is a serious matter. Have you recognized its effects upon you? What happens when you keep pushing and pushing without coming back into balance?

....

....

....

....

....

....

9. On a regular basis, you need to have times when you get replenished, and that may require you to say no to some requests and to disappoint a few friends or family members. Describe a time when you said yes when you knew you should say no and it took a big toll on you.

> *If you're living overdrawn, you'll be overwhelmed when the next big withdrawal hits.*

....

....

....

....

....

....

....

10. During the pandemic or during another season of your life when you had to change your schedule and slow down for some reason, did you get a new perspective on what your priorities for living should be? What changed for you?

....

....

....

....

....

....

11. When you're pushing yourself hard and running at a deficit, are you more depleted emotionally, spiritually, or physically? What area is affected the most?

....

....

....

....

....

12. Read 2 Corinthians 1. The apostle Paul had made a commitment to visit the church at Corinth, but what two unexpected challenges came up? As powerful and resilient as Paul was, what did he have to tell the Corinthians? Even though they were expecting him, and even though Paul knew they needed him, what did he have to do first?

....

....

....

....

....

....

13. Jesus and Paul both learned to say, "No, sorry, I can't do it now. I have to get refreshed." It's okay if you do it too. Name some specific things that you know you should be saying no to, but you're still trying to be Superman.

....

....

....

....

....

....

14. What valuable lesson can you take from the successful pastor who pushed himself beyond the breaking point?

....

....

....

....

....

....

15. It's easy to blame others for an overbusy schedule, but you make your schedule. Take some time and reflect on where you are overcommitted. What is that busyness doing to you?

....

....

....

....

....

16. Advertisers, television, the Internet, social media, school, work, family, and friends are vying for your attention. What do you need to be more selective about what you commit to? What can you change right now that will allow for some replenishing?

> *Good things can wear you out. Good people can deplete you. It's all about balance.*

....

....

....

....

....

17. Solomon wrote about a woman who said, "My brothers were angry with me; they forced me to care for their vineyards, so I couldn't care for myself—my own vineyard" (Song of Solomon 1:6 NLT). If you could have a talk with her, what advice would you give her?

....

....

....

....

....

....

18. How does the story of the lighthouse keeper summarize the main lesson of this chapter? What is the one purpose for which you have been given oil?

....

....

....

....

....

....

....

....

....

....

19. Too many people are burning out. You can go for a while living out of balance, but eventually it will catch up to you. Based upon what you've learned in this chapter, what new perspectives are you taking from now on? Write a bold declaration of your commitment to living balanced.

....

....

....

....

....

....

....

....

....

....

....

....

Stay connected, be blessed.

Get more from Joel & Victoria Osteen

It's time to step into the life of victory and favor that God has planned for you! Featuring new messages from Joel & Victoria Osteen, their free daily devotional and inspiring articles, hope is always at your fingertips with the free Joel Osteen app and online at JoelOsteen.com.

Get the app and visit us today at JoelOsteen.com.

 Joel | **JOEL OSTEEN** MINISTRIES

CONNECT WITH US